BARBADOS
Ah Come From
Dem Did De Days & Other Bajan Poems

by

Osbert Wilton McClean, BJH

BARBADOS
Ah Come From
Dem Did De Days & Other Bajan Poems

by

Osbert Wilton McClean, BJH

PUBLISHER'S NOTES

Published by Osbilproductions

Paperback Edition (5.5 x 8.5)
ISBN: 978-976-96010-0-0

Other Editions: *Thinking Thoughts Book Series.*

These are:
Adventures of Poor Frankie Volumes 1, 11 & 111
Daddy Girl
Mummy's Darling Daughter
Celebration Independence Time

Copyright © 2016 by Author: Mr. Osbert McClean

*Book Design and Text Composition by
Grafixx 2 Inc: info@grafixx2inc.com*

ABOUT
THE AUTHOR

OSBERT WILTON MCCLEAN was born in Barbados in the parish of St. Philip. He was a dramatist and was the founder and Director of the Princess Margaret Cultural and Dramatic Group (PRIMCADA). He taught for 36 years as a History Teacher with his last teaching post being at the Princess Margaret Secondary School.

During his lifetime, he wrote literary works for several persons in Barbados. These literary works have won silver and gold awards at the National Independence Festival of Creative Arts (NIFCA). He also travelled across parishes in Barbados helping to establish cultural and dramatic groups. For many years he organised the cultural component of the Oistins Fish Festival, which is held annually in the historic fishing village in Oistins, Christ Church, Barbados. He was the author of the **Thinking Thoughts Book Series** which comprises of:

Adventures of Poor Frankie

Volumes 1, 11 & 111

Daddy Girl

Mummy's Darling Daughter

This book **Barbados Ah Come From** was started prior to his passing in November 2019. It reflects the history of Barbados through a compilation of his poems and is a commemoration of one of his lifetime goals of ensuring the history of Barbados was preserved for generations to come in an artform that would be appealing to many people. On the occasion of Barbados' 50th Independence anniversary, he was one of the fifty Barbadians to be awarded the Barbados Jubilee Honour for his outstanding contribution to education and culture.

Forever Remembered
Lisa Mcclean-Trotman, PhD
(Daughter)

Table of Contents

Dem
did de days

Dem did de days
When de days were the days.
In those days
You remember those days Sammy Boy?

The days of the dry cane stump?
The cow dung that filled the dung basket?
The crocus bag in your lap and the apron?

De days you would go down underneath
The big mahogany tree down in the woods
For the seeds for your coal pot and heater
To press yuh clothes.

The rotten cane.
The cane peeling.
De coffee fence tree and de dry-pea tree
To build paling for your backyard
And wood to cook de food.

You set on de big buck pot
On top of three red bricks in de yard.
You drew the match
And dash in a bit of dry trash.
See how the fire burn
Pretty fuh so.

Hot and red
Up into de sky
Especially when you threw
Some kerosene oil here and there.
Fire! Fire! Pretty fuh so.
Hot and hotter!
Brighter and brighter!

Den de rain would come down.
The smoke!
The smoke reached high and higher
Up into de sky.
In your nose and in your eyes
Making your eyes red, red, red.
Water came down into your mouth
Salty, salty, salty.

Don't mind the eyes burning.
You never worried that the ashes slipped down your throat
and on to your palate
To mek you cough.

But never mind the coughing.
You knew your food would be cooked with
real Bajan flavour
When you tasted the smoke in the boiled back dumpling
Too hard and tough to bite them.

The okra slush with pieces of the thick salt fish
and eddoe leaf in it
On top of the mellow "engine" corn cou-cou.
Slimy, but sweet doh neh.
So delicious and tasty it made your mouth water.
The flying fish with the mustard bush or spinach rice
Lathered down with brown flour sauce,
You could stay down by the prison and smell it!

De split-pea mutton soup seasoned up wid barley
And de green pawpaw.
You know pawpaw good fuh de pressure?
De big pot of stew potatoes,
Eddoes – they itched you neh?
You threw them out in a dung basket;
You took a chunk of roast salt fish
All welcome de potato and de eddoe
Enough and lots to spare.
So take your share.
De pone that would be made out of cassava flour;
De homemade coconut bread
That would tire out your jaw.

Dem did de days.
When in those days
Lots of fish were in fashion.
The conk shell blew and blew
It would deafen your ear.
You ran outside;

Everybody around the fish cart:
Dolphin, red snapper, jacks and frays
The flying fish
Plenty and cheap.
You scaled some.
You roasted some.
You fried some.
You steamed some.
You salted up some.

Don't tell me that you forget the fish that used to be left
On top of the roof to dry in the sun?
They burnt your tongue!
No electricity.
No fridge.
All that money saved.
Meat was no problem either in those days.
De days of the corned mutton;
The corned pork;
The touched-pork with the smell.
You never bothered because de taste was de ting
Oh what a taste!

Den you washed down with a large tot of mauby.
And the lemonade
You would drink and drink
Until yuh belly filled up to yuh mouth
And you would lie down on the floor and roll and roll.

Dem did de days

When in those days
You didn't know
Anything about radio or television.
The coolie man's credit was enough.
No sale! No low down payment racket!

Shoes were luxuries for the "poor great" and the wealthy.
Don't mind the chigoe or your heels full of holes;
Walking barefoot was no shame.
The flour bags made pretty jiffy dye shirts'
The "drawers" the nightgowns too
Saved the old, the young lots of shame
And hid the nakedness.

The days of yard fowls, the ducks, the turkey,
The rabbits, the cows, the goats
And the sheep you grazed by the roadside.
Every morning and on evenings
You picked your rabbit meat and cut your bag of grass.
But now all of that is done.
All of that is done.

Dem did de days! Dem did de days!

You ever cleaned out a pig-pen yet? The smell!
Oh the smell that don't care how much perfume or blue
soap you used
You still had that smell.
But that smell paid for the term fees
When they tried to educate dem to bring them out of dem
days
And stop dem from smelling hell in these days.
And now they say that they forgot dem that brought dem
out of dem days.
Saying that dese days are their days.
These are their days?

Are they really their days?

Don't ever forget the ones that brought us out of dem
days.

Thank the Lord I am still alive

I woke up early this morning.
Thank the Lord I am still alive.

Washed my skin in a bucket of cold water.
Thank the Lord I am still alive.

Scrubbed my teeth with some bicarbonate soda.
Thank the Lord I am still alive.

Set on the butter skillet of water to make my tea.
Thank the Lord I am still alive.

The sky blue chocolate tea cocoa or coffee.
Thank the Lord I am still alive.

A couple of hard biscuits with some butter.
Thank the Lord I am still alive.

Left the dirty water to soak down in soap water.
Thank the Lord I am still alive.

Slipped on the slippers on my feet and tied up my waist.
Thank the Lord I am still alive.

Scarcely time to comb or plait my hair... I had to haste.
Thank the Lord I am still alive.

No time to lose because the clock hands at ten to six.
Thank the Lord I am still alive.

So the children left with their own breakfast to fix.
Thank the Lord I am still alive.

Some stew potatoes, salt fish cakes, muffins for me.
Thank the Lord I am still alive.

It is only at weekends all of my children I can see.
Thank the Lord I am still alive.

I work hard from sunrise to sunset.
Thank the Lord I am still alive.

I have to cut and contrive with the little wages I get.
Thank the Lord I am still alive.

Tired around my waist and in my knees.
Thank the Lord I am still alive.

When I got home outside so dark I could hardly see.
Thank the Lord I am still alive.

Washed out the clothes; by midnight food done cook.
Thank the Lord I am still alive.

The roasting cassava, breadfruit, dumplings too.
Thank the Lord I am still alive.

Green banana Cou cou and kiddy-dip stew.
Thank the Lord I am still alive.

Everyone fast sleep as soon as the last spoonful done.
Thank the Lord I am still alive.

On the Khus-Khus grass bed on the floor we lie down.
Thank the Lord I am still alive.

The loud snores of hard work of a stressful day.
Thank the Lord I am still alive.

We sleep strong, wake up early next morning to pray.
Thank the Lord I am still alive.

Another day of hard work and endless care.
Thank the Lord I am still alive.

We are still alive? I am still alive to survive.
Thank the Lord I am still alive.

Those
Days of
Hard Wuk

Those days of hard wuk
When they had no luck,
Working for a little bit of money;
To recall those days, it seems so funny,
To lots of young folks today.
But we will talk and tell it as we may,
And don't care: really don't care,
What nobody says! No way!

We remember well,
They saw enough of hell
As they tried to make ends meet.
Many a day, nothing to eat,
But they bravely stood the test,

So we could survive, just like the rest.
They did their best,
They really did their best.

They worked all day,
For hardly any pay,
From sunrise to sunset,
Through hot or cold, dry or wet.
Oh what a pitiful sight!
They worked at times, until late at night,
To bring us out of that plight,
What a struggle they had to fight!
They really had to fight.

So I am telling you all now,
Listen carefully to how they spent those days.
To know where we will be,
The past we must see,
So don't be ashamed to hear,
Because we should know, how they lived,
And due respect to them give.

Servant Work Once Upon a Time

Once upon a time,
Servant work was easy to find.
From minding the missus children,
To washing the clothes, ironing and cooking.
Making up the beds, scrubbing the floor.
It was work and work and much more.
From six in the morning until eight at night you wuk.
Thursday half-day occasionally, if you had any luck.

One Sunday a month you got as an 'off- day'.
And if you took sick one day; you got no pay.
You worked your 'soul-case' off for missus.
If she overworked and underpaid you; you made no fuss.

But when she gave you the beef, mutton or chicken
To cook, you boiled it first and drink the 'broth' to
strengthen your body.
The drink of whisky! You took the first sip
From the glass you're taking to her; then add some water
to it.

Yes, once upon a time,
Doing servant work wasn't any crime.
Servant and missus usually got on well.
All her hidden secrets you she would tell.
You were her confidante when her husband went astray.
Just imagine the negative things about him she would say.
Then you knew why she married such a misfit man like
him.
Unmarried and having a baby in her family was a
disgraceful sin.

Of course, once upon a time,
Relationship with servant girl and mistress was not always
fine.
Take for instance what happened to a friend of mine
Who went one day to a mistress hoping servant work to
find.
Dressed in seersucker, lavender blue skirt, taffeta blouse,
Stepping in spike -heel shoes in style she reached the
house.
Red and blue maroon 'pork- chop' pocket- bag under her
arm too.
Not even "King Dyal" in all his glamour, her could he
outdo.
Hear her: "Missus Bleary, please Madam Missus Bleary,
I come all the way from up the way in the country;
To see if I can get the job in the papers, that you advertise.
Mistress you got to give me the job, please; otherwise

I don't know how my children and me going to survive,
true.
My mother and my old grand-mother are depending on
me too.
Without this job, all of us will soon suffer from 'pot fever',
yes.
To satisfy and please you at all times, I will try my best."

"Tell me young lady, what qualifications do you possess?
Can you cook to suit me? My husband's clothes press?
The last maid I had here didn't even know when water
boiled.
And once when baking the cake in the oven she
'endorsed, it with lard oil.
You see, many of you young girls nowadays can't do one
thing,
But 'dress up' in the latest fashion and fancy hair-styles
sporting.
As we slip through the door for work you're on our phone
gossiping.
Week after week our 'price gouged' groceries supply, is
lessening."

"Missus Bleary, anything you ask I can do.
I can stir a delicious pot of mellow Indian corn coucou.
The okra slush brown flour sauce gravy with the thick salt
fish.
Or red herring or mackerel and roast sweet potatoes, what
a dish!
The boiled-back cassava, guinea corn dumplings, in 'belly
soup', too.
Clean your house from room to room, spick and span to
please you.
And all of your clothes I will wash 'clean as a whistle', true,
true.

Wash stiff starch and iron, like how my grand mother
taught me to do.”

“Well to help alleviate your poverty the job to you I will
give.
Twenty dollars a week and in the maid’s room you can live.
You will baby-sit for me when I go out at night too.
And any favour my husband requests, you will have to
do.”

“Missus Bleary, you hold your ‘horses’ right there for me!
Although I might be in need of a job you aren’t exploiting
me.
Before I work for ‘next skin to nothing’ at any body like
you,
I will pick cotton, a dollar a pound. Good bye! Your work
you can do!”

25 DEACONS ROAD

De Bus-stand Hawker

Popcorn, toffees or mint!
Look, here's your sweet child Cint.
Nuts, fresh a fresh
Good for the flesh
The best straight from the pan
Right here into the bus stand.
Crispy and not too brown,
Buy a pack or a quarter pound.

The sugar cakes, the comforts, firecatch!
Delicious sweet-biscuits have no class or match.
Don't mind the times hard
These biscuits got in nuff lard.
I don't have to tell you twice

They taste really really nice.
The glassies - none other can test;
Everything here is top-class and the best.

Hey saga boy, you will feel like a king in the land
When you put a pack of nuts in the girlfriend's hand.
Popcorn, toffees, sugar cakes and mint!
Surely you are going to buy from sweet girl Cint.

Wait what happened to you? Yes I mean you;
You want me to sin my soul today? No can do.
You want a sample? For these you intend to pay?
Boy move from here and take your hand out of my tray.

Bajan
Market Scene

Oranges, bananas, get the juicy grapefruit!
The sweet oranges! The yellow meat breadfruit!
The plantains five for a ten dollar;
These figs are really tasty to swallow.

Wait young fellow, you said my thing are too dear?
Well buy from somebody else. Please yourself hear.
Young lady you say you want a bunch of my thyme?
Well you see those seasonings there? Those too are mine.
You have to buy a pound of seasoning from me
If you want an ounce of my thyme, see?

Why we hawkers so "thieving so" you can't see yet?
Look when you all go to the supermarket
And you see the price tag do you question it?
No you put the items fast in a trolley and you go along
Don't check if the weight and price, are right or wrong,
But you come asking me why my price so dear?

Well let me tell you straight from my heart
Before I sell you my produce for next-skin-to- nothing
They will stay in my tray and rotten.
These prices vat free – don't make any fuss
Get the peas and guinea corn to make jug for Christmas.

Yes sir, come here. All my produce grows locally.
Don't take her on Sir, mine are the best! Believe me.
This is called breadfruit Sir; Tasty locally dish;
Try some with some pickled souse and salt fish.
Proper tasty bajan meal for you and the family, see?
Price sir? Two cost five dollars US currency.
Want some tania, eddoes and sweet potatoes too?
Move Kimpadoo! The gentleman wants me not you!
You talking to me Kimpadoo?

**Oranges, grapefruit, the bananas, okras and yellow
meat breadfruit!**
I am selling two for five dollars and a quarter!
Who's that saying that my oranges sour?
But why this man don't leave me in peace though?
What I got for him very soon he will know.
What's that you said Elmira? I'm not hearing you right?
As you are ready girl; we will sleep in prison tonight.
Come back here Sir! Buy from me not from her;
Buy one orange for two fifty and get one free.
Thank you very much Sir. Here you are very welcomed
indeed.

**Get the bananas, the sweet oranges and grapefruit!
The okras, limes, squash and the tasty breadfruit!**

Did
you ever?

Did you ever walk from Bathsheba to
Bridgetown?
Oh that was great fun!
Picked 'wilts' late at night on the rocks by the
sea?
Oh what a joy that used to be for my friends and
me.
'Sucked' sugar cane 'butts' in cane planting
Season in November?
What pleasant juicy thoughts of joy to
remember!

Did you ever ever play 'hiddy biddy' shut up
your lap tight, tight?
Fun galore it was on a bright full moon night.
And what about 'corking' or 'puss, puss catch a
corner'?
How happy we were playing near the street
corner.

Did you ever play hopscotch, warri and potter?
With roast corn played 'a bundle of bush how many men
on deck'?
Drink lots of water when you done! What fun you sure bet.
Oh how I wish those days again we would get!

Did you ever used to catch lizards with a 'slip me noose?
Or with a cane blade set fly-stick, wood-doves to catch ?
Or a 'gutter perk' made?
You know what I am talking about though? Oh no!
Well ask Granny or Grand-daddy, they surely should know.
But you ever played 'hide and hoot' in sour grass
And trash heap?

Tell me, you ever on a moving cane-truck hopped
And leaped?
You ever spun a top and sent it to sleep yet?
Or played lagging with kite?
What about, playing 'London Bridge is falling down',
And other games at night?
Full moon! Every body having innocent laughter and fun.
Nobody, having to be afraid of gangs with knife
Cutlass or gun!

Did you ever dare to misbehave yourself or curse
And swear in public?
And a sound thrashing by any adult you didn't get?
Go home to complain to parents, would you dare to do?
Seriously! I would be sorry for your backside and you.

You ever realized the joy and fun our fore parents had?
Then why can't we?
You think we would ever?
Never, ever? Never, ever get back there again?

Proud
To Be A Bajan

Are you not proud to be a Bajan?
Loyal sons and daughters of this lovely island.
With beautiful beaches; wonderful scenery,
Welcoming visitors with warm loving hospitality.

I don't know about you; I am confident about me;
I am proud to be Bajan. I love and adore my country.
That is why I am excited to celebrate with much glee
Barbados independence anniversary.

So if you are feeling proud to be a Bajan like me;
Then let us all join together and say lustily:
Happy birthday Barbados! Happy anniversary!
We are proud to be independent and free.

We love Barbados and with pride and industry.
Our national anthem we will sing and raise for all to see.
Our beautiful flag with colours black, gold and blue,
We are proud to say Barbados we love you.

Independence means a lot to me

Independence means a lot to me,
I am free and so is my beloved country.
We are free to chart our own destiny
And we do it with great pride and industry.

If independence means to you what it means to me
And you believe we are truly free,
Then let us join hands together and joyfully celebrate
November 30th – our country's birthdate.

It was nineteen sixty – many years ago
Errol Walton Barrow – the first Prime Minister – our hero
At the Garrison took the salute as our flag
Blue, black and gold replaced the union jack
and in the air flew.

It was really a time to remember I am told,
The rejoicing! The fireworks! What a sight to behold.
So let's heartily rejoice again; be happy! Make merry
Thank God we are independent and free! Be happy.

Happy birthday beloved country Barbados.
Happy anniversary from all of us.
We shall join hands, heart and voice
Let us lustily shout, make merry rejoice.

Let us hold our national flag high and honour
Our national anthem as we sing and repeat our motto
Pride and industry. We are glad to be free
Independence really means a lot to me.

Glossary of Terms

B
Buck pot: A big wide pot usually made out of iron

C
Crocus bag: A sack made from finely knitted brown cord used in the old days for carrying produce to and from the market or to and from the plantation

Coucou: A local dish made from cornmeal okra and hot water

Comforts: A sweet mint-like candy

Corned pork: A way of preserving pork with salt in the absence of a refrigerator

Corned mutton: A way of preserving sheep meat (lamb) with salt in the absence of a refrigerator

D
Dung basket: A big basket used for carrying manure or for carrying the cane buck when planting canes

Drawers: The name that was given to underwear worn by older women that was made out of white cotton

F

Flour bags: A cloth bag used to keep flour. Some persons used the bag to make clothing

Fire catch: A sweet confectionary that is made from sugar

G

Glassies : A sweet confectionary that is made from sugar

K

Khus-Khus grass: A type of grass used around the caneground to prevent soil erosion during the cane ground. Some people used Kuss Kuss grass as padding for beds

N

Next-skin to nothing: An expression that means to sell item with very little or no profit

O

Okra slush: A gravy made from okra and saltfish

P

Paling : A fencing that it made from old galvinise

Pressure: A bajan word used for hypertension

S
Sugar cakes: A sweet confectionary that is made from sugar, coconuts and spices

W
Wuk: Barbadian dialect word that means work

Y
Yard fowls: Chickens that were reared in one's backyard

Osbert McClean is one of Barbados's prolific writers. This collection of poems capture key aspects of Barbados culture and history through the years and reminds us of our rich heritage.

Memories such as sucking cane, hopping on the cane truck, catching lizards with slip me noose; going into the Bridgetown Saturday mornings to listening to the hawker selling in the bus stand are all captured in the poems in this book.

Through his unique writing style the smell, sights and conversations of the past are all captured in a captivating and entertaining way.

A must read for those who not only want to reminesce but who want to ensure that the younger generation never forget this island's rich heritage.

This body of work is truly barbadiana...it paints a picture of village life as seen through the eyes of a man who skillfully used language that is easy on the tongue and images that one can close one's eyes and taste, feel and hear Barbados. I hope this makes its way into the libraries and classrooms.

- Carl Alff Padmore (Poet and Dramatist)

These writings beautifully captured bajan life in the early years in Barbados and paints vivid pictures that triggered memories of my past.

- Stedson E. Wiltshire, D.Litt, BSS, BJH (Cultural Ambassador, Barbados)

ISBN: 978-976-96010-0-0